The Devil's Advisory Council

Iblees ki Majlis-e-Shoora

THE DEVIL'S ADVISORY COUNCIL

MUHAMMAD IQBAL

Translated by Abdussalam Puthige

The Other Press
Kuala Lumpur

Published by
The Other Press Sdn. Bhd.
607 Mutiara Majestic
Jalan Othman
46000 Petaling Jaya
Selangor, Malaysia
www.ibtbooks.com

The Other Press is affiliated with Islamic Book Trust.

Perpustakaan Negara Malaysia   Cataloguing-in-Publication Data

Muhammad Iqbal, 1877-1938
      The Devil's Advisory Council: Iblees Ki Majlis-e-Shoora 1936/
      Muhammad Iqbal; Translated by Abdussalam Puthige.
      ISBN 978-967-0957-15-9
      1. Urdu poetry. 2. Poets, Urdu.
      I. Puthige, Abdussalam. II. Title.
      891.43915

Printed by
SS Graphic Printers (M) Sdn. Bhd.
Lot 7 & 8, Jalan TIB 3, Taman Industri Bolton
68100 Batu Caves, Selangor Darul Ehsan

The Author
Allama Muhammad Iqbal
(1877-1938)

Sir Muhammad Iqbal, also known as Allama Iqbal and Dr Iqbal, was one of the 20th century's greatest poets, philosophers and leaders. He was born in Sialkot, Punjab. His ancestors were Kashmiri Brahmins who had embraced Islam some three centuries previously. After completing his early education in Sialkot, Iqbal moved to Lahore where he graduated from the Government College. He then earned his masters degree in philosophy and English literature at the Oriental College. He later rejoined Government College of Lahore, this time as a lecturer in philosophy, history and literature. He started writing poetry in Urdu at a very early age. His work was noted for its depth and versatility. During his days in the Government College of Lahore, he was in touch with such eminent literary figures as Sir Thomas Arnold.

In 1905, Iqbal travelled to Europe to pursue higher studies. He was awarded a scholarship to Trinity College in Cambridge, England and obtained a Bachelor of Arts (BA) degree in 1906. The same year, he was admitted to the Bar as a barrister by Lincoln's Inn. Later, Iqbal moved to Germany and earned his PhD, under the supervision of Friedrich Hommel, from the Ludwig Maximilian University, Munich, in 1908. 'The Development of Metaphysics in Persia' was the title of his doctoral thesis.

Apart from England and Germany, Iqbal visited other countries in Europe and met many scholars, writers and political leaders. In Spain, he visited Cordoba (Qurtuba) and offered prayers at the historical Masjid e Qurtuba. This visit is said to have had a great influence on him. In Italy, he met Mussolini. During his stay in Europe, Iqbal began writing poetry in Persian.

In 1908, Iqbal returned to Lahore and started practicing law. At the same time, he devoted much of his time to literary activities and played an active role in politics too. He was a member of Anjuman-e-

Himayat-e-Islam, an organization dedicated to promoting education in the Muslim community. In 1919, he became the general secretary of this powerful organization. He was conferred knighthood in 1922. In 1927, he was elected as a member of the Punjab Legislative Assembly. He presided over the annual session of the Muslim League in 1930 and attended the Round Table Conference, held in London, to frame a constitution for India.

Iqbal wrote seven books in Persian and four in Urdu.

One of the most important themes evident in the works of Iqbal is *khudi*, translated as 'individuality', 'self', 'self-hood', and interpreted as 'self-awareness', 'self-confidence', etc. This concept was first expounded by Iqbal in his long, didactic poem *Asrar-e-Khudi* (Secrets of the Self), which he wrote in 1915. In 1920, it was translated into English by R.A. Nicholson, who had been his examiner at Cambridge. It is a great honor for a pupil to have his book translated by his professor. Professor Nicholson's translation introduced Iqbal and his philosophy to Europe.

The second theme visible in Iqbal's philosophy is the need for constant change, evolution, action and movement. He would not tolerate stagnancy, inaction and immobility even in heaven.

The third theme evident in his works is the battle between *'ishq'* and *'aql'* or Love versus Reason wherein the former has been glorified and the latter depicted as the villain.

Iqbal accorded Man a very high position and discussed in detail the role of Man in the scheme of existence. Rejection of imperialism, capitalism, materialism and nationalism are also constant themes in Iqbal's works.

Iqbal is known by many titles such as *Allama* (scholar par excellence), *Shayir-e-Mashriq* (Poet of the East), *Mufakkir-e-Islam* (Ideologue of Islam), *Hakeem-ul-Ummah* (Wise Man of the Community), etc. He is considered as one of the greatest poets of all times both in Urdu and Persian languages. He was noted for his in-depth knowledge of Arabic, Persian and European literature.

Apart from the Holy Qur'an, the life of prophet Muhammad (s) and his companions, he was profoundly influenced by Jalaluddin Rumi, the legendary Persian poet and sufi sage of the 13th century, and some Western philosophers such as Friedrich Nietzsche, Henri Bergson and Goethe.

His first Urdu book in prose *'Ilm al-Iqtisad* (The Science of Economics) was written in 1903. Iqbal's poetic works are written mostly in Persian. Among his 12,000 verses of poem, about 7,000 verses are in Persian. His first poetic work *Asrar-i-Khudi* (1915) was followed by *Rumuz-i-Bekhudi* (1917). *Payam-i-Mashriq* appeared in 1923, *Zabur-i-Ajam* in 1927, *Javid Nama* in 1932, *Pas cheh bayed kard ai Aqwam-i-Sharq* in 1936, and *Armughan-i-Hijaz* in 1938. All these works were in Persian. The last one, published posthumously is mainly in Persian except for a few poems and ghazals in Urdu.

His first book of poetry in Urdu, *Bang-i-Dara* was published in 1924, followed by *Bal-i-Jibril* in 1935 and *Zarb-i-Kalim* in 1936.

A collection of his English lectures and letters titled '*The Reconstruction of Religious Thoughts in Islam*' was published by Oxford Press.

Iqbal was a close and trusted associate of Muhammad Ali Jinnah, the founder of Pakistan.

The Translator

Abdussalam Puthige (b. 1964) is a journalist, author, translator, speaker, trainer and a social activist. He graduated in history from ICE, University of Madras, studied law at SDM Law College, Mangalore, and did his postgraduate studies in human rights at the Indian Institute of Human Rights, New Delhi. He is the chief editor of *Vartha Bharathi*, a popular Kannada daily newspaper published simultaneously from Bangalore and Mangalore. He is the founder and director of Madhyama Kendra, a Bangalore based NGO engaged in media related studies, research and training.

Puthige has authored six books in Kannada and three in English, and has translated over a dozen books mainly from Urdu to Kannada. His recent work, *Kannadadalli Qur'an Anuvada*, a translation of the entire Qur'an in Kannada with brief notes, is widely acclaimed for its simple, chaste and lucid style. First published in 2012, it has already seen six editions. Its third edition was published by the Ministry of Islamic Affairs, Dubai, UAE. His internationally acclaimed work *Towards Performing Da'wah* (1998) was published by the International Council for Islamic Information, Leicester, UK, in 1998.

His English translation of Allama Iqbal's renowned work *Shikwa aur Jawab-e-Shikwa* was published by Islamic Book Trust, Malaysia and was released in Dubai in 2015.

Puthige studied Urdu, Arabic and Islamic theology under his father the late Maulana Muhammad Shafi'i, and studied Persian literature under the late Maulana Sayyed Muhammad Yunus.

Preface

Sir Dr Muhammad Iqbal (1877-1938) is one of the greatest legends of the subcontinent. The incredibly rich legacy of the powerful thoughts he left behind in the past century continues to influence and inspire millions of hearts and minds till today and will continue to do so for a long time to come. His poetry is either in Urdu or Persian and both are enriched with Arabic and Qur'anic elements. However, due to the inherent beauty of his message and its universal appeal, his works have reached and influenced humanity in almost all parts of the planet.

Shikwa aur Jawab-e-Shikwa and *Iblees ki Majlis-e-Shoora* are considered to be among his most celebrated works.

Iblees ki Majlis-e-Shoora is believed to be written by Iqbal during the last phase of his life (1936). Many, who are familiar with the previous writings of Iqbal look at this work as his concluding remarks over all the works of his lifetime. This poem in fact presents the essence of his message to the modern world in general and to the Muslim community in particular.

It is significant that while, in all his other works, Iqbal has tried to convey the message of God through the statements of God, in this particular work, he delivers God's warning to mankind against the evil designs of *Iblees*, through the mouth of the latter.

Iblees ki Majlis-e-Shoora consists of 64 couplets presented in the form of a conversation between *Iblees* and the five members of his advisory council. *Iblees* presides over the entire session and leads the conversation. His views are packaged in 34 couplets, 6 in the form of opening remarks and 28 in the form of conclusions. In between, his 5 trusted advisers air their views.

A review of the story of *Iblees* or *Shaitan* (Satan) as narrated in the Qur'an would help readers better understand the theme in *Iblees ki Majlis-e-Shoora*.

According to the Qur'an, when Adam (*a*) was created, all the angels and the jinn were commanded to prostrate before him, *Iblees* in his arrogance refused to do so. He was not ready to accept either the superiority of Adam (*a*) or that of mankind. "I am better than him (Adam)", he proclaimed (Qur'an, 7:12). At a later stage, he was successful in misleading Adam (*a*) by luring him to defy a crucial command of God. When he was being thrown out of heaven, he made an appeal to God. "Allow me respite till the day they are raised up (i.e. the day of resurrection)." Allah said: "You are of those allowed respite." (Qur'an, 7:14-15).

Ever since, *Iblees* along with his comrades are engaged in a full-time global mission of misleading humanity. His goal is to induce human beings by any means into disobeying their Lord. *Iblees* believes that it was because of Man that he lost the high position he enjoyed in paradise. He is now determined to avenge this loss by depriving all human beings of any opportunity to enter paradise. Benefiting fully from the respite granted by God, he is busy contriving sinister plots one after the other to deceive mankind. Every success encourages him to emerge with more sophisticated conspiracies and every defeat provokes him to indulge in more determined onslaughts. Therefore, partly at least, human history has been the history of *Iblees* cleverly laying traps and humanity imprudently walking into them. God does provide guidance to mankind but does not compel them to follow it. *Iblees* constantly presents his own deceptive road maps to people to keep them away from the divinely prescribed path of success. He makes people believe that the paths prescribed by him will lead them to truth, justice, fraternity, peace, harmony and prosperity. But those who trust him and peddle his path are doomed to end up in total falsehood, injustice, destitution, anarchy, conflict, bloodshed and mass destruction. *Iblees* celebrates this calamity as his success.

In *Iblees ki Majlis-e-Shoora* Iqbal exposes this scheming in the form of boastful claims straight from the mouth of *Iblees*. We are witnesses to a back room meeting, in which *Iblees* and his advisers arrogantly assess and evaluate their clandestine plans and conspiracies – past, present and future.

Iblees, presiding over the session, initiates the proceedings by boasting about his successful experiments with imperialism and capitalism. He says "On the one hand, I was successful in endearing capitalism and imperialism to the hearts and minds of the rich and powerful ruling class, and on the other, I was able to persuade the masses to meekly bow before the capitalists and the imperialists without any resistance. For this purpose, I created the idea of fatalism. Through the philosophy of fatalism, I induced the masses to believe that they were born to serve the rich and the monarchs and that there was nothing in their destiny except submission and servitude. They voluntarily submitted to the will of the affluent and the rulers without ever thinking of their own interests, rights or dignity. This helped both the capitalists and the imperialists to enslave many successive generations over the centuries, without facing any resistance".

A debate follows. The first adviser in the council enthusiastically endorses the claims of *Iblees* and adds a few statements in his support. He says that due to their belief in fatalism, the masses have lost even the ability to desire freedom. Mullahs (scholars, priests) and sufis (mystics), instead of educating the masses and leading a revolt, have proclaimed their own loyalty to the monarchs. He explains how, due to the conspiracies of *Iblees*, many crucial practices prescribed by Islam were detached from the true spirit behind them and became mere rituals.

The second adviser does not seem to agree. He is worried about a new challenge that was raising its head universally — the challenge of the so called 'rule of the masses' or democracy. He tells the first adviser, "You are not aware of the potential of this ideology."

The first adviser consoles him by affirming that democracy was nothing but imperialism in disguise. "After centuries of suffering under imperialism, when Man began to show some signs of prudence, we presented monarchy before him, packaged in an attractive form. We do not really need a king or a monarch to run our regime. After all, what matters is the spirit and the spirit prevailing behind democracy is not much different from that of imperialism."

The third adviser says: "If democracy is really not much different in substance from the age-old imperialism, then we need not worry at all. But then, what about the threat posed by the philosophy of Karl Marx? It might lead people to revolt against their enslaving masters."

The fourth adviser reassures the third adviser, "There is really no need to worry about the Marxist challenge. The modern-day heirs of the old imperial Roman lords, nourishing the dreams of enjoying the kind of power their ancestors did, are seasoned enough to take care of this threat."

Referring to the rising tides of the fascist movement led by Mussolini in Italy, he says that the successors of the great Roman empire have with them an effective antidote to deal with Karl Marx and his ideas.

The third adviser partly agrees with this argument and says that although Mussolini has exposed the political system of Europe, he is not a great visionary.

The fifth adviser, instead of speaking to the members in the council, directly addresses *Iblees* and shares his concern and apprehensions about the Marxist ideology. After showering praises on *Iblees* and equating him with God, he says he is afraid that the wicked world raised by *Iblees* through his unique wisdom might fall victim to the fire of equality ignited by Marx.

Finally, *Iblees* delivers his presidential remarks in 28 couplets. This is the longest and most crucial part of this poem. To begin with, *Iblees* reaffirms his total faith and confidence in his own wicked wisdom, his manipulative powers and his well-knit network of evil. Dismissing all the threats pointed out by his advisers, he says the evil empire raised by him was too strong and stable to be threatened by any religion or philosophy. Only idiots, he claims, would underestimate the strength of his empire. He boasts, he can always fool the political leaders and the spiritual masters. He vilifies the socialists by calling them bread hunting vagabonds incapable of causing any damage to his empire.

Finally, he comes to the crux of the matter unveiling what he is really fearful of. Pointing towards the Muslim ummah or the global Muslim community, he says that herein lies the real threat to his empire. While he is very happy with the current, sad state of affairs of the community, he is afraid of the great revolutionary potential hidden in this community. He enumerates the unique benefits Islam offers to humanity and the radical transformation it can bring about in the lives of the people. Then he suggests various techniques to keep Muslims away from the essence of Islam.

Iblees
The Devil

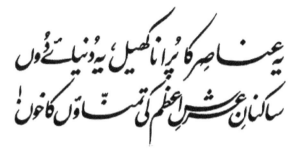

Ye anasir ka purana khel, ye dunya-e-doon
Saakinaan-e-arsh-e-azam ki thamanaon ka khoon!

This wretched world, this age-old game of elements,
shattering the ambitions of the dwellers
of the great divine throne![1]

---

[1] *Iblees* is referring to the angels. He says that, the angels wanted the post of *Khalifa* (Vicegerent of God) for themselves. But, with the entry of Man, all their dreams were shattered.

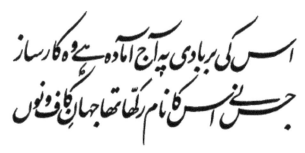

Uski barbaadi pe aaj aamada hai woh kaarsaaz
Jisne uska naam rakha tha jahaan-e-kaaf-o-Noon.

That very Creator is today bent upon ruining it,
Who once had named it 'the world of *K* and *N*'[2].

---

[2] According to the Qur'an, existence in its entirety came into being in response to one brief command of God. He said "*Kun*" meaning *Be*. (In Arabic, this word "*Kun*" consists of two letters, *Kaaf* and *Noon*). And in response, the universe came into being. See the Qur'an: "The Originator of the heavens and the earth! When He decrees a thing, He says unto it only: Be! and it is." (2:117)

2

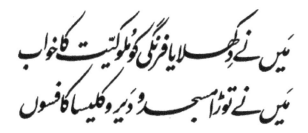

Maine dikhlaya farangi ko mulookiyath ka khwaab
Maine thoda masjid-o-dair-o-kalisa Ka Fasoon

I inspired in the European the dream of imperialism:
I broke the spell of the mosque,
the temple and the church.[3]

---

[3] Referring to secularism, the instrument used to separate
the state from the church (or religion) and thereby to
deprive the state of all moral and spiritual values.

میں نے ناداروں کو سکھلایا سبق تقدیر کا
میں نے منعم کو دیا سرمایہ داری کا جنوں

Maine naadaaron ko sikhlaya sabaq taqdeer Ka
Maine mun'im ko diya sarmayadari ka Junoon

I taught the lesson of destiny to the destitute[4]
I gave the rich the passion of capitalism.[5]

---

[4] Fatalism is a distorted and degenerated form of faith in destiny. It leads people to meekly accept all forms of injustice and oppression in the name of destiny. It deprives them of optimism and any trust in their own ability to bring about any change.

[5] Capitalism engenders greed and the belief that true success comes from amassing wealth using every possible means, without bothering about any moral value or responsibility.

See Qur'an: "...who collects wealth and keeps counting it. He thinks that his wealth will make him immortal..." (104:2-3)

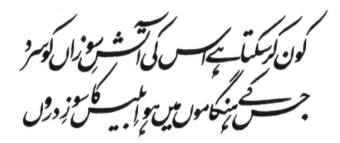

Kaun Kar Saktha Hai Uski aathish-e-soozan ko sard
Jis Ke hangamon mein ho Iblees ka souz-e-daroon

Who can ever cool down the fire blazing in him?
In whose frenzied uproar,
is hidden the fire storm of *Iblees*.[6]

---

[6] *Iblees* tries to strengthen the confidence of his associates by telling them that the empire of evil created by him is too deep-rooted to be dismantled by anybody.

جس کی شاخیں ہوں ہماری آبیاری سے بلند
کون کر سکتا ہے اُس نخلِ کہن کو سر نگوں !

Jis ki shaakhen hon hamari aabyari se buland
Kaun kar saktha hai us nakhl-e-kuhan ko ser nigoon!

Who can ever bend down that age-old tree?
Whose branches have grown so high
because we have watered it![7]

---

[7] *Iblees* makes these tall claims only to reassure his associates. In fact, he knows that his empire is too feeble to stand the scrutiny of the truth. The Qur'an says: "Indeed, the plot of Satan has ever been weak." (4:76)

Pehla Musheer
The First Adviser

Is mein kya shak hai ke muhkam hai ye Ibleesi Nizam
Pukhta thar is se huwe khoo-e-ghulami mein awaam.

No doubt, this system of *Iblees* is quite stable,
It has hardened masses in their servitude.[8]

---

[8] *Iblees* has been successful in instilling a deep sense of pessimism in the minds of the masses, so much so, that betraying their own interests, they have given up resistance against the oppression by the wicked powers and have accepted slavery as their destiny.

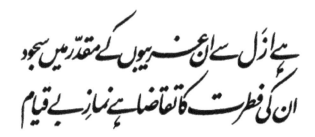

Hai azal se in gharibon ke muqaddar mein sujood
In ki fitrat ka thaqaza hai namaz-e-be qayaam.

Mere prostration has been the fate of these
poor masses since the beginning of time,
Their nature is such that standing up
is not a part of their *namaz*.[9]

---

[9] In fact, the act of *namaz* (*salah*) that every Muslim is obliged to perform five times a day involves various postures including standing, bowing down, falling in prostration and sitting on the ground. All these acts symbolize his readiness to obey the divine command under all circumstances. However, according to *Iblees*, Muslims have accepted prostration as their only fate and have lost their ability to stand up.

ارزواول تو پیدا ہو نہیں سکتی کہیں

ہو کہیں پیدا تو مرجاتی ہے یا رہتی ہے خام

Aarzoo awwal tho paida ho nahin sakthi kahin
Ho kahin paida tho mar jaathi hai yaa rehethi hai kham.

Any desire (for freedom) cannot emerge
in them anywhere, in the first place,
Perchance if it does, either it dies down
or remains hollow.[10]

---

[10] Obviously, desire for freedom is the first step to attain freedom. When a nation or community has lost the ability to desire freedom, how can it be expected even to fight for it?

یہ ہماری سعیِ پیہم کی کرامت ہے کہ آج
صوفی و ملّا مُلوکیت کے بندے ہیں تمام

Ye hamari saee-e-peham ki karamath hai ke aaj
Sufiomullah, mulookiyath ke bande hain thamaam.

This is the marvel of our persistent efforts that today,
sufis and mullahs alike are the slaves
of the monarchs.[11]

---

[11] Traditionally sufi mystics and scholars of Islam have been the prime sources of guidance and inspiration for the Muslim community. The first adviser in the council of *Iblees* says that this community has lost both these sources. Those who were supposed to lead the movement for justice and equality have chained themselves to the slavery of the ruling masters. Hence, there is no possibility of any revolt or rebellion by this community.

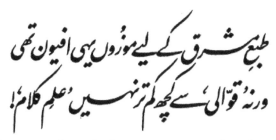

Taba-e-mashriq ke liye mauzoon yehi afyoon thi
Warna 'Qawwali' se kuch kam thar nahin 'ilm-e Kalam'

This was the opium quite apt for the
temperament of the East,
Or else, *ilm-e-kalam* (scholastics) is in fact,
not any less futile than the *qawwali*.[12]

---

[12] *Qawwali* is a form of devotional music popular in
the subcontinent. The adviser says that the Muslim
community has fortunately engaged itself debating trivial
theological issues. They are not aware that these debates
are as futile as *qawwali*.

بے طوافِ و حجّ کا ہنگامہ اگر باقی تو کیا
کُند ہو کر رہ گئی مومن کی تیغِ بے نیام

Hai thawaf-o-hajj ka hangaama agar baqi tho kya
kund ho kar reh gayi moomin ki thaigh-e-be nayam.

So what if the clamour of the rituals
such as *tawaf* and hajj do remain,
(Because) the unsheathed sword of the Believer
has lost its edge.[13]

---

[13] According to this adviser of the *Iblees*, the Muslim community, despite all the plots of *Iblees*, has not abandoned its religion. However, he draws solace in the fact that Muslims have retained mere rituals and have lost the revolutionary spirit of their faith. Although they do practice some formal acts of worship, they no longer are aware of jihad, or their universal duty to fight for justice and equality and to resist all forms of injustice and exploitation.

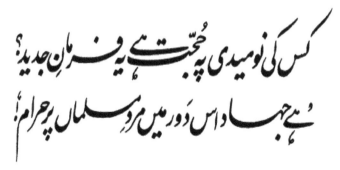

Kis ki naumeedi pe hujjath hai ye farmaan-e-jadeed
'Hai Jihad is daur mein mard-e-musalman par haraam!'

'Jihad is prohibited on the Muslim men of this era',
Whose gloom does this
modern-day proclamation manifest?[14]

---

[14] During the peak of colonial rule, at the behest of the ruling masters, many Muslim scholars in several colonized countries had begun to issue *fatwas* proclaiming that jihad is prohibited for Muslims of the modern era. The adviser says, these proclamations clearly indicate that the community stands utterly frustrated and such a community can never pose any threat to the evil regime of *Iblees*.

Doosra Musheer
The Second Adviser

Khair hai sulthani-e-jamhoor ka ghogha ke sharr
Tu jahan ke thaaza fithnon se nahin hai ba-khabar!

Is this uproar of 'rule of the masses'
(democracy) good, or is it bad?
You are unaware of the novel mischiefs
of this world![15]

---

[15] The second adviser thinks the first adviser is not wise enough to read the situation in the right manner. He believes that the latter has failed to take note of the emergence of democracy which is the real challenge to the empire of *Iblees*.

Pehla Musheer
The First Adviser

Hun, magar meri jahan beeni bathathi hai mujhe
Jo mulookiyath ka ek parda ho, kya us se khathar!

Indeed, I am aware, but I am guided
by my experience of this world,
There is no danger at all in that which
is a mere cloak of monarchy.[16]

---

[16] Now the first adviser pacifies the second by informing him that democracy in its essence is not radically different from imperialism. There is no reason to look at democracy as a threat. After all, it is nothing but the same old imperialism wrapped in an attractive cloak.

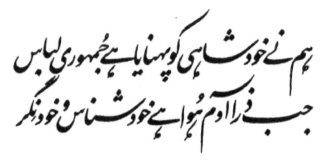

Hum ne khud shahi ko pehnaya hai jamhoori libas
Jab zara Adam huwa hai khud shanaas o khud nigar.

When Man grew up and to some extent,
began to be aware of himself,
No one else but we disguised monarchy
in the garb of democracy.

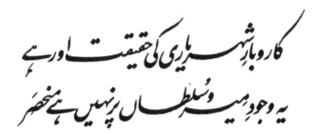

Karobaar-e-sheheryari ki haqeeqath aur hai
Ye wujood-e-meer-o-sultan par nahin hai munhasar.

The essence of imperialism is quite unique,
It does not depend upon the existence
of any leader or monarch.

مجلسِ ملّت ہو یا پرویز کا دربار ہو
ہے وہ سلطاں، غیر کی کھیتی پہ ہو جس کی نظر

Majlis-e-millat ho ya Parvez ka darbar ho
Hai woh Sultan, ghair ki kheti pe ho jis ki nazar.

Whether it is the peoples' council or
the court of *Parvez* (the ruler of Persia),
He who covets the garden of the other,
is indeed the king.

تُو نے کیا دیکھا نہیں مغرب کا جُمہوری نظام
چہرہ روشن، اندُروں چنگیز سے تاریک تر!

Thu ne kya dekha nahin maghrib ka jamhoori nizam
Chehra roshan, androon Changez se thaareek thar!

Have you not seen the
democratic system of the West?
Its face looks bright, but internally it is
darker than the rule of Chengez (Genghis Khan).[17]

---

[17] Externally, democracy in the West seems to be so immensely benevolent and so much in the interest of the masses. However, on close scrutiny it turns out to be more oppressive than the brutal rule of Genghis Khan, the notorious Mongol king of the 13th century who brutally massacred millions.

Teesra Musheer
The Third Adviser

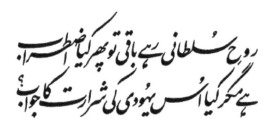

Rooh-e-sultani rahe baqi tho phir kya iztaraab
Hai magar kya us yahoodi ki shararath ka jawab?

We have no reason to panic as long as
the spirit of imperialism is intact,
But, does anything match the mischief
of that shrewd Jew?[18]

---

[18] The reference is to Karl Marx. The third adviser appears to be happy to know that democracy is not a threat to the empire of *Iblees*. But he has his apprehensions about the rising tides of Marxism.

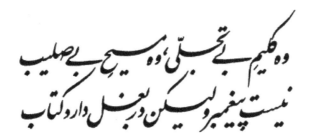

Woh kaleem be-thajalli, woh maseehe be-saleeb
Neesth paigambaro lekin dar baghal daarad kithab.

He is Moses (*a*) without the miracles and
Jesus (*a*) without the cross,
Though not a prophet,
he carries a book under his arm.[19]

---

[19] Referring to *Das Kapital* of Karl Marx.

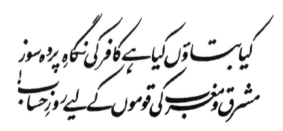

Kya bathaun kya hai kafir ki nigah-e-parda souz
Mashriq-o-maghrib ki qaumon ke liye roz-e-hisab.

How can I explain the power of the
piercing vision of that infidel!
It is doomsday for the nations
of both the East and the West.

اِس سے بڑھ کر اور کیا ہوگا طبیعت کا فساد
توڑ دی بندوں نے آقاؤں کے خیموں کی طناب!

Is se badhkar aur kya hoga thabiyath ka fasaad
Thod di bandon ne aqaaon ke khaimon ki thanab!

What will better manifest the
devastation of human nature?
The slaves have severed the ropes
of their masters' tents.[20]

---

[20] Influenced by Karl Marx and his philosophy, the working
class began to revolt against its traditional masters. The
adviser points this out to prove his point that Marxism is
the most formidable challenge facing the *Iblees* regime.

Choutha Musheer
The Fourth Adviser

توڑ اس کا رومۃ الکبریٰ کے ایوانوں میں دیکھ
اٰلِ سیزر کو دکھایا ہم نے پھر سیزر کا خواب

Thod iska roomatul kubra ke aewanon mein dekh
aal-e-Ceaser ko dikhaya hum ne phir Ceaser ka khwaab.

Look for its antidote in the palaces
of the great Roman empire.
We have revived the Caesar's dream
in the progeny of Caesar.[21]

---

[21] Referring to Benito Mussolini of Italy and his ideology,
fascism.

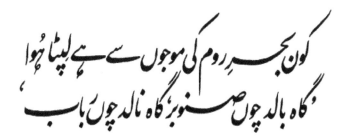

Kaun behr-e-room ki maujon se hai lipta huwa
'Gah baalad choon sanobar, gah naalad choo rabab'.

Who remains engulfed in the waves
of the Mediterranean?
'At one moment, it grows like a giant pine and
at the next, it meekly wails like a *rebab*'.[22]

---

[22] *Rebab* is a musical instrument that resembles the lute.

Teesra Musheer
The Third Adviser

Mein tho us ki aaqibath beeni ka kuch Qael nahin
Jis ne afrangi siasat ko kiya yun behijab.

I'm not satisfied with his farsightedness.
Who has so effectively exposed
the politics of Europe.[23]

---

[23] The third adviser acknowledges the might of fascism. In fact, the fascist movement exposed the anti-semitism that was hidden deep inside the hearts and minds of the so-called liberal European nations. The remarkably fast growth of fascism and the consequent bloodbath witnessed

throughout Europe exposed the vulnerability of the 'liberal' traditions of the West. However, at the same time, he says that he is not convinced that Mussolini and his philosophy will be able to defeat Marxism in the long run.

Panchwan Musheer
(*Iblees Ko Mukhatib Kar Ke*)
The Fifth Adviser
(addressing *Iblees*)

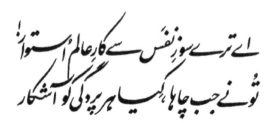

Ae therey souz-e-nafas se kaar-e-aalam usthwaar!
Thu ne jab chaha, kiya har pardagi ko aashkaar.

It is the warmth of your breath that
keeps the affairs of this world stable,
You have unveiled every hidden fact,
whenever you have wished to do so.

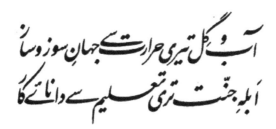

Aab-o-gill [24] *theri haraarat se jahan-e-souz-o-saaz*
Abla-e-jannat theri thaaleem se danaye kaar.

Thanks to your efforts, this earth has
become a hub of beauty and actions,
And thanks to your guidance, the innocuous of the
paradise[25] (Man) has become master of skills.

---

[24] *Aab-o-gill* (water and clay) indicate the earth.

[25] The fifth adviser reassures *Iblees* that he is far superior to both the angels and the human beings. According to him, by stupidly trusting *Iblees* and running into the trap laid by him and consequently depriving himself of all the privileges he once enjoyed in paradise, Man has proved to be too naïve a being. If he is master of many arts and skills today, credit should go to *Iblees* for teaching him those arts and skills.

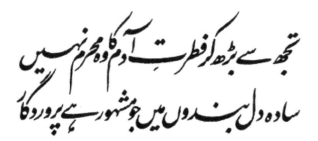

Tujh se badhkar fithrath-e-adam ka woh mehram nahin
Saada dil bandon mein jo mashoor hai parwardigaar.

The one known as God among the innocent masses,
Does not know the human nature,
better than you do.[26]

---

[26] The fifth adviser goes a step further and places *Iblees* above God. He says, "You understand human nature much better than the one known to innocent masses as God."

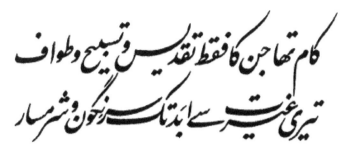

Kaam tha jin ka faqat thaqdees-o-thasbeeh-o-thawaf
theri ghairat se abad thak sar nigun-o-sharmsaar.

Those (angels) who were always preoccupied in
mere praising the Lord, glorifying Him
and running in circles,
Are in eternal remorse and hang their heads
in shame before your pride.[27]

---

[27] Obviously, the reference is to the angels.

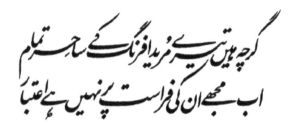

Garche hain thereymureed afrang ke saahir thamaam
Ab mujhe un ki firaasath par nahin hai aithebar.

All the spellcasters of Europe are
your disciples though,
I no longer trust their sagacity.

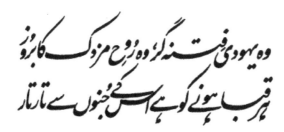

Woh yahoodi fitna gar, woh rooh-e-Mazdak ka barooz
Har qabaa hone ko hai uske junoon se thaar thaar.

That mischief mongering Jew,
that personified the spirit of Mazdak[28],
his fanatic zeal is about to tear apart every robe.

---

[28] Mazdak (died circa 524AD) was a Zoroastrian priest, Iranian reformer and religious activist who claimed to be a prophet of Ahura Mazda. He is believed to have promoted the concept of collective ownership and introduced several social welfare programmes. His Mazdaki cult is considered as a heresy in Zorostrianism. Many see him as a socialist of his times. Here the reference is again to Karl Marx and his socialism.

زاغِ دشتی ہو رہا ہے ہمسرِ شاہین و چرغ

کتنی سرعت سے بدلتا ہے مزاجِ روزگار

Zagh-e-dashti ho raha hai humsaar-e-shaheen-o-chargh
Kithni sur'at se badalta hai mizaaj-e-rozgar.

The wretched crow is vying to be at par
with the falcon and the hawk,
Look, how fast the temperament of
the times change.[29]

---

[29] Referring to the rapid rise of communism or Marxism, the fifth adviser says that the poor and the wretched of the earth have begun to claim rights and privileges at par with the feudal lords and the rich barons.

34

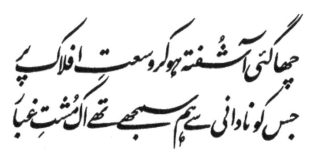

Cha gayi ashufta ho kar wusa'at-e-aflaak par
Jis ko nadani se hum samajhe the ek musht-e-ghubar.

But today, it has become restless and
has totally occupied the skies,
In our ignorance, we had considered this
as a mere handful of dust.

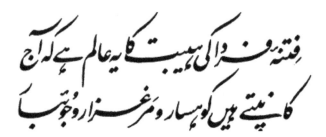

Fitna-e-farda ki haibat ka ye aalam hai ke aaj
kanpthe hain kohsar-o-murghzaar-o-joo'ay baar.

The fear of the future crises is so dominant today,
the mountains, the gardens and the streams
are all trembling in horror.

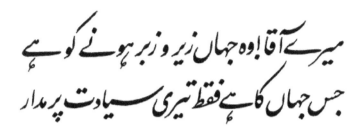

Mere aaqa! woh jahan zair-o-zabar hone ko hai
Jis jahaan ka hai faqath theri sayaadath par madaar.

My Lord, that world is about to be upside down,
Which depends totally on your hegemony.[30]

---

[30] The fifth adviser concludes his remarks by airing his
serious concern about the radical change being brought
about in human thought by Marxism and warns *Iblees* that
it might ultimately ruin his evil empire.

Iblees (Apne Musheeron Se)
Iblees (to his Advisers)

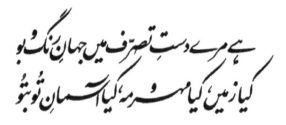

Hai mere dast-e-thasarruf mein jahan-e-rang o bu
Kya zameen, kya mehar o mah, kya aasman-e-thu ba thu

This world of colours and scents
is totally under my command,
the earth, the sun, the moon and
every layer of the sky included.

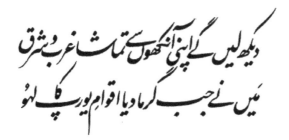

Dekh lenge apni aankhon se thamasha gharb-o-sharaq
Mainey jab garma diya aqwam-e-Europe ka lahoo.

Both the East and the West shall witness
the spectacle with their own eyes,
When I would have boiled the blood
of the European nations.

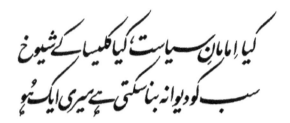

Kya imaamaane siasat, kya kaleesa kay shuyookh
Sabko deewana bana sakti hai meri aik hoo.

Whether they are pioneers of politics
or theologians of the church,
A single sigh of mine can drive crazy one and all.

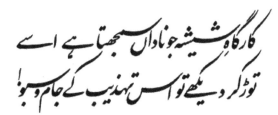

Kaargah-e-sheesha jo naadaan samjhta hai use
Thod kar dekhe tho is thehzeeb ke jaam-o-saboo!

The fool who thinks all this is a mere work of glass,
Let him try to break the pots and cups
of this civilization and he will see.

دستِ فطرت نے کیا ہے جن گریبانوں کو چاک
مزدکی منطق کی سوزن سے نہیں ہوتے رفو

Dast-e-fithrat ne kiya hai jin garebanon ko chaak
Mazdaki mantaq ki souzan se nahin hote rafoo.

The collars torn by the hands of nature,
The needle of Mazdak's logic[31] will
never be able to stitch together.

---

[31] Here, 'the needle of Mazdak's logic' indicates the ideology or philosophy of materialism. *Iblees* says that natural disparities will always remain and that the materialist philosophy will never be able to erase them.

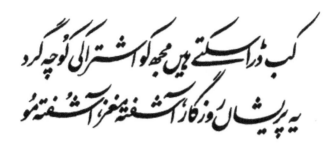

Kab daraa sakthe hain mujh ko ishtharaaki koocha gard
Yeh pareshaan rozgaar, aashuftha maghz, aashuftha Hu.

How can these socialist vagabonds ever scare me?
They are mere bread hunters,
with derailed thoughts and incoherent speech.

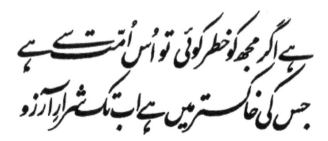

Hai agar mujh ko khathar koyee tho us ummath se hai
Jis ki khakistar mein hai ab thak Sharar-e-aarzu.

If at all I apprehend any threat,
it is from that community[32]
which has in its ruins,
a spark of ambition even today.

---

[32] Referring to the global Muslim community.

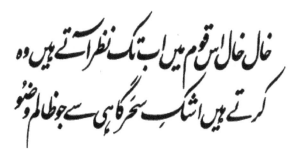

Khaal khaal is qaum mein ab thak nazar aathe hain woh
Karthe hain ashk-e-sehargahi se jo zalim wuzoo.

Although rare, even to this day
such are found in this community.
Who do their *wuḍū'*[33] using the tears they
shed during their predawn supplications.

---

[33] *Wuḍū'* is the ritual partial ablution performed prior to
salah or prayers at least five times a day.

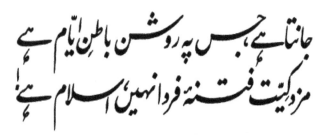

Jantha hai, jis pe roshan baathin-e-ayyaam hai
Mazdkiath fitna-e-farda nahin, Islam hai!

Anybody who knows the secrets
of the current era is aware,
That the future threat to my system lies not in
Mazdakism but in Islam.

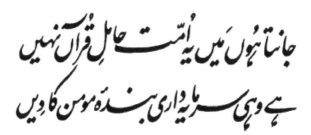

Jaantha hun main yeh ummat haamil-e-Quran nahin,
Hai wohi sarmayadaari banda-e-momin ka deen.

I am aware that this community
no longer upholds the Qur'an,
The believer has embraced capitalism as his faith.

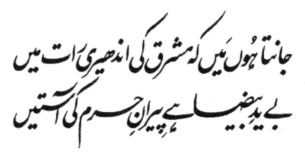

Janta hun main ke mashriq ki andheri raath mein
Be yad-e-baiza hai peeran-e-haram ki aastheen.

I am aware that in the dark night of the East,
The old leaders of the *Haram*[34] stand, with no
sparkling hand[35] under their sleeves.

---

[34] *Haram* is the restricted area around 'Masjid al-Haraam'
in Makkah. The boundary of the *Haram* starts about 3
miles away from Makkah, in the direction of Madinah and
7 miles each from Makkah on the road to Yemen, at-Ta'if
and Iraq respectively and 10 miles away on the road to
Jeddah.

[35] Reference is to the sparkling or luminous hand, one of
the mighty miracles gifted to Musa (*a*). Musa (*a*) without
the sparkling hand would be a weak entity, unable to face
the giant forces of the Pharaoh. *Iblees* here equates the
modern-day Muslim community to Musa (*a*) without his
sparkling hand.

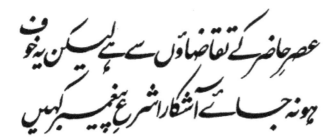

Asre-e-haazir ke thaqaazaon se hai lekin yeh Khauf
Ho najaaye aashkara shara-e-paighambar kahin.

Demands of the modern era
lead me to the apprehension,
That the law of the prophet might get disclosed.[36]

---

[36] Every age will have its own needs and challenges. *Iblees* says that the needs of the modern era and the challenges facing it are such that in the process of addressing them, this era is likely to end up at the doorsteps of Islam.

الحـــــذر! آئین پیغـــمبر سے سَو بار الحذر
حافظِ ناموسِ زَن، مردِ آزما، مردِ آفـــریں

Alhazar! Aaeen-e-paighambar se sau baar alhazar!
Hafiz-e-naamoos-e-zan, mard aazma, mard aafreen.

Beware, a hundred times beware,
of the law of the prophet,
It guards the honor of the woman,
challenges the men's might and
is the mentor of true men.[37]

---

[37] "Men are the protectors and maintainers of women." (Qur'an, 4:34)

"And what is (the matter) with you that you fight not in the cause of Allah and (for) the oppressed among men, women, and children who say, 'Our Lord, take us out of this city of oppressive people and appoint for us from Yourself a protector and appoint for us from Yourself a helper?'" (Qur'an, 4:75)

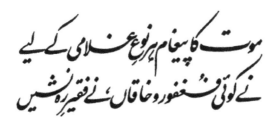

Mauth ka paighaam har nau-e-ghulami ke liye
Na koyee faghfoor-o-khaaqaan,
nay faqeer-e-reh nasheen.

It is a message of death for every kind of slavery,
Neither will there remain the kings and
emperors nor any wretched destitute.

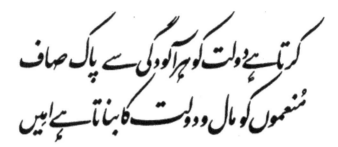

Kartha hai doulat ko har aaludgise paak saaf
Mun'imon ko maal-o-daulath ka banata hai amen.

It purifies the wealth from every impurity,
It makes the wealthy, mere custodians of the wealth.[38]

---

[38] "Wealth and children are an ornament of life of this world. But the good deeds which endure are better in thy Lord's sight for reward and better in respect of hope." (Qur'an, 18:46)

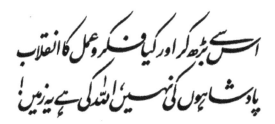

Is se badhkar aur kya fikr-o-amal ka inqilaab
Padshahon ki nahin, Allah ki hai yeh zameen!

Can there ever be a greater revolution
of thought and action (than this?)[39]
This earth belongs to Allah and
not to the monarchs.

---

[39] "Unto Allah belongs the sovereignty of the heavens and
the earth. Allah is able to do all things." (Qur'an, 3:189)

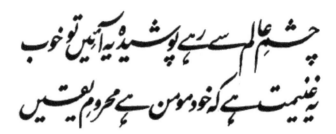

Chashme aalam se rahey poshida ye aaeen tho khoob
Ye ghaneemath hai ke khud momin hai
mehroom-e-yaqeen.

Better, this code remains concealed
from the sight of the world,
Fortunately, the believer himself
is deprived of *yaqeen*.[40]

---

[40] Absolute conviction. Contrary to this statement of *Iblees*,
Allah commands in Qur'an: "And cover not the truth with
falsehood, nor conceal the truth when you know it." (2:42)

یہ ہے یہی بہتر الہیات میں الجھارہے
یہ کتابُ اللہ کی تاویلات میں الجھارہے

Hai yehi behthar elaahiyath mein uljha rahe
Ye Kitabullah ki thaweelath mein uljha rahe.

Better it is that he remains entrapped in theology,
And always remains entangled
interpreting the Book of Allah.[41]

---

[41] He (Allah) it is Who has sent down to thee the Book: In
it are verses basic or fundamental (of established meaning);
they are the foundation of the Book: others are allegorical.
But those in whose hearts is perversity follow the part
thereof that is allegorical, seeking discord, and searching
for its hidden meanings, but no one knows its hidden
meanings except Allah. And those who are firmly
grounded in knowledge say: "We believe in the Book; the
whole of it is from our Lord: and none will grasp the
message except men of understanding." (Qur'an, 3:7)

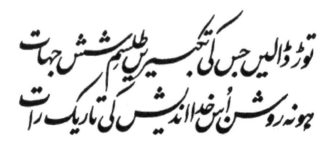

Thod daaleen jis ki thakbeerain thalism-e-shash jihaath
Ho na roshan us khuda andaish ki thareek raath.

His cry of *Takbīr* [42] broke the spell that had occupied
all the six directions (the universe),
Make sure, the dark night of this
God conscious Man never turns bright.

---

[42] Glorifying Allah.

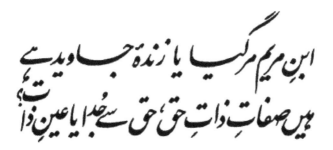

Ibne Mariam mar gaya ya zinda-e- jaaved hai
Hain sifath-e-zaath-e-haq, haq se judaa ya ayn-e- zaath?

Did the son of Mary die, or is he eternally alive?[43]
Are the attributes of God distinct from God
or do they constitute God's own self?

---

[43] "That they said (in boast), 'We killed Jesus Christ the son of Mary, the Messenger of Allah' — but they killed him not, nor crucified him, but so it was made to appear to them, and those who differ therein are full of doubts, with no (certain) knowledge, but only conjecture to follow, for of a surety they killed him not." (Qur'an, 4:157)

اے آنے والے سے مسیح ناصری مقصود ہے
یا مجدّد جس میں ہوں فرزندِ مریم کے صفا

Aane wale se maseeh-e-naasiri maqsood hai
Ya mujaddid, jis mein hon farzand-e-Mariam ke sifaath?

Who really is meant by 'the awaited'?
Is he the Messiah (Jesus) of Nazareth?
Or a reviver, who has in him the qualities
of 'the son of Mary'[44]?

---

[44] "So peace is on me the day I was born, the day that I die, and the day that I shall be raised up to life (again)!" (Qur'an, 19:33)

"Such (was) Jesus the son of Mary: (it is) a statement of truth, about which they (vainly) dispute." (Qur'an, 19:34)

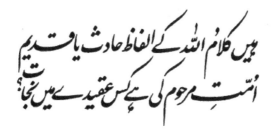

Hain kalaamullah ke alfaaz haadis ya qadeem
Ummath-e- marhoom ki hai kis aqeede mein najaath?

Are the words in the Book of Allah
temporal or eternal?
Which set of beliefs would lead the
blessed community (Muslims) to salvation?[45]

---

[45] "When you see people engaged in vain discourse about Our signs, turn away from them unless they turn to a different theme. If Satan ever makes you forget, then after recollection, do not sit in the company of those who do wrong." (Qur'an, 6:68)

کیا مسلماں کے لیے کافی نہیں اس دَور میں
یہ الہیّات کے ترشے ہوئے لات و مناتؔ؟

Kya musalman ke liye kaafi nahin is daur mein
Ye ilaahiyath ke tharshay huwe laath- o-manaath?

Will these not be sufficient in this age
to take care of the Muslims,
These idols (*Lāt* and *Manāt*)[46]
carved out by theology?

---

[46] Objects of worship popular in Makkah before the revelation of the Qur'an. *Iblees* says that just as the people of those times whose obsession with these false gods had kept them away from the message of truth, so we should ensure that the Muslims of the current era remain obsessed with trivial theological issues. These issues assume the role of false gods and keep the Muslims far away from the revolutionary message of their true God.

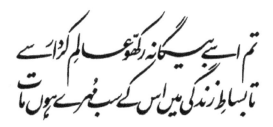

Thum use begaana rakho aalam-e-kirdar se
Tha Bisaath-e-zindagi mein is ke sub muhrey hon math.

Make sure he remains indifferent to character,[47]
So that every move of his, on the board of life,
turns out to be disastrous.

---

[47] The Prophet (s) said, "The most complete of the believers in faith are those with the best character, and the best of you are the best in behavior to their women." (Narrated by Abu Huraira (ra), Tirmidhi, 1162.)

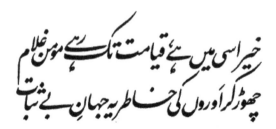

Khair isi mein hai, qayamat thak rahe momin ghulaam
Chodkar auronki khatir ye jahan-e-be-sabaath.

It is in our interest that the believer
remains enslaved till the end of times.
Leaving this temporal world,
at the disposal of others.

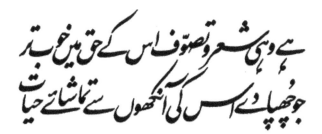

Hai wohee sher-o-thasawwuf us ke haq mein khoobthar
Jo chupa de us ki aankhon se thamaasha-e-hayaath.

The same old poetry and
mysticism is good for him,
That leaves his eyes unable
to see the realities of life.

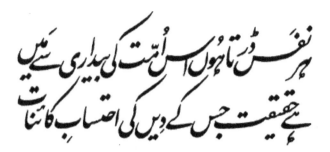

Har nafas dartha hun is ummath ki bedari se mein
Hai haqeeqath jis ke deen ki ehtisaab-e-kaainaath.

I am always scared of this community being aware,
Reckoning the universe[48] is the
true spirit of their faith.

---

[48] By 'reckoning the universe' *Iblees* means two inherent universal duties incumbent on every Muslim. First, his global social responsibility of striving to establish justice, promote virtues and prevent evil. Second, his duty to seriously ponder over all the phenomena found in this universe.

"Do they not look at the camels, how they were created? And at the sky, how it was raised high? And at the mountains, how they were firmly set? And at the earth, how it was spread out?" (Qur'an, 88:17-20)

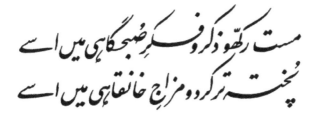

Masth rakho zikr-o-fikr-e-Subhgaahi mein usay
Pukhtathar kar do mizaaj-e-khaanqahi mein usay.

Keep him ever occupied in ritual chants and
contemplation during the predawn hours[49],
Make him all the more seasoned
in *Khanqah*[50] temperament.

---

[49] While Islam persuades people to frequently remember
Allah and contemplate over His creation, it warns them
against being ritualistic and adhering to mere ritual
practices. There have been many sects and cults in the
history of the community that have bound people to
hollow rituals in the name of spirituality. Ritual spiritual
exercises prescribed by these cults virtually meant escape
not only from their social responsibilities but from realities
of life too. Those who walked into this trap were left with
neither any interest nor any time for striving to establish
justice in the society.

[50] *Khanqah* is the sufi counterpart of the monasteries that symbolize self-imposed seclusion and total escape from all the worldly affairs, in the guise of spiritual pursuit.

9 789670 957159